OH LORD, WHY *Me?*

OH LORD, WHY *Me?*

Meditations that Encourage and Challenge Your Faith in this Strife-Ridden World

Editors:
Rev. Dr Joseph A. Conner & Evangelist June A. Conner

Suffolk, Virginia

Oh Lord, Why Me?
Meditations that Encourage and Challenge Your Faith in this Strife-Ridden World

Copyright © 2020 by
Dr. Joseph A. Conner and June A. Conner
All rights reserved.

All rights reserved. This book is protected by the copyright laws of the United States of America. This book may not be copied or reprinted for commercial gain or profit. The use of quotations or occasional page copying for personal or group study is permitted and encouraged. Permission will be granted upon request.

Final Step Publishing, LLC
PO Box 1441
Suffolk, VA 23439
www.finalsteppublishing.com

Soft cover ISBN: 978-1-7355280-6-9

For Worldwide Distribution. Printed in U.S.A.

Contents

Acknowledgments   7

Introduction   9

Part One: Lord, I'm Stressed!

1. Living Through a Spiritual Pandemic   13
   Joseph A. Conner Sr.

2. It was Unexpected, I was not Ready!   17
   June A. Conner

3. GPS   21
   Audrey E. Moody

4. A Sound Mind!   25
   June A. Conner

Part Two: Lord, I'm Weary!

5. I'm Tired of Being Tired   31
   Joseph A. Conner Sr.

6. This is Not the Time!   37
   Marsha Brown Woodard

7. Life Happens   41
   June A. Conner

8. I Can't Breathe.   45
   Joseph A. Conner

Part Three: Lord, I Need Your Power!

9.   Deliverance from Disappointment   51
Joseph A. Conner Sr.

10.   God is Present in the Storm!   57
Patricia A. Blount

11.   Watch Out!   61
Audrey E. Moody

12.   Waiting for Morning!   65
June A. Conner

Part Four: Lord, I Need Your Help!

13.   Handling Life's Detours   71
Joseph A. Conner Sr.

14.   Decisive Decision Making   75
Robert E.C. Jones Jr.

15.   Serving One Another   79
June. A. Conner

16.   Like Rizpah   85
Audrey E. Moody

Acknowledgments

The writing of a book requires many gifts from many servants of the Lord. I want to express my thanks and gratitude to my gifted wife, June, for her dedication and devotion to the completion of this project.

It is because of the confidence of Bishop Joseph D. Clemmons that I was afforded the opportunity to become an officer of the Hampton University Ministers' Conference. I have had the awesome privilege of serving and being tutored by these past Presidents of the conference: Rev. Dr. William H. Curtis, Ambassador Susan Johnson-Cook, Bishop Claude Alexander, Rev. Dr. Dwight Riddick, Rev. Dr. Robert Perry, and Rev. Dr. ACD Vaughn.

I am thankful for the prayers and nurturing of Bishop O.T. Jones Sr., Bishop O.T. Jones Jr., Bishop Benjamin J. Ravenel Sr., Bishop Robert L. Hargrove, Bishop Ernest C. Morris Sr., Rev. Doris Sherman, Rev. Dr. Delrio Berry, Mother Anna Brown, and Deacon John and Mother Christine Avent. They all are a part of my village from the Church of God in Christ (COGIC).

Giving honor to Bishop Guy L. Glimp, who is the leader of the Pennsylvania Commonwealth Ecclesiastical Jurisdiction. My parents, Rev. Joseph Conner and Mother Margaret J. Conner and my uncle, Rev. William E. Green Sr. have been my physical and spiritual parents.

My local church family, the New Beginnings-Sanctuary of Praise COGIC and the family of my spiritual birth, Holy Temple COGIC of Philadelphia, have supported me with love and prayers.

To each of the ministers who have contributed their written thoughts of inspiration to this publication, thank you. I appreciate my brothers by another mother who have been sources of encouragement: Bishop Nathan Baxter, Rev. Guy Craig Davis, Rev. Nathaniel Goodson, Deacon Ronald Johnson, and Brother Ralph Gordon.

To God be the Glory!

Introduction

Introduction

Dr. Conner, affectionately known as The Rabbi, serves faithfully as the pastor of New Beginnings Church of God in Christ and the Chief Adjutant of the Pennsylvania Commonwealth Ecclesiastical Jurisdiction under the leadership of Bishop Guy L. Glimp. He is an Overseer at Large in the National Adjutancy of COGIC, as well as an active member of the Black Clergy of Philadelphia and Vicinity.

In *Oh Lord, Why Me?*, Dr. Joseph Conner has gathered some unique writers who work and minister to those who are in crisis or dealing with strife in their lives as well as those individuals seeking a deeper walk with God. In this book, our writers have shared painful personal experiences, words of encouragement, and have offered reflective meditations to those of us that are living through these extremely trying times. COVID-19, racism, stress, illness, and grief are all around us. It can often lead us to lose track of who is in control.

Dr. Conner and our writers have laid bare their struggles, deep frustrations, and challenges; sharing how they were able to recover from these life-changing situations and move forward through the grace of God and the move of the Holy Spirit. Topics covered in this book: "What to do when stressed, when weary, in need of God's power, and in need of God's help," are expressed in such a way that will uplift, inspire, empower, and challenge you as you deal with the hazardous trials of life.

Our title, *Oh Lord, Why Me?*, comes from the exclamation that many of us utter when out of nowhere life takes the hand of fate and knocks us to the ground.

Dr. Conner has always been described as a preacher who has a heart for people. His last book, *Sound the Alarm!*, detailed the crisis occurring in our communities due to the large numbers of incarcerated African Americans and the problems and stresses caused by an unjust penal system and the churches' response to that problem. This book focuses on the individual in crisis to stem the assault on our physical and spiritual lives by the enemy. It is our hope that as you read this, you will be encouraged that with God's help, you can make it!

June A. Conner

PART ONE:
Lord, I'm Stressed

Constantly projecting, "what if," would only raise my stress levels and make my situation worse. The question, "Oh Lord, why me?" just added to that stress!

Evangelist June A. Conner

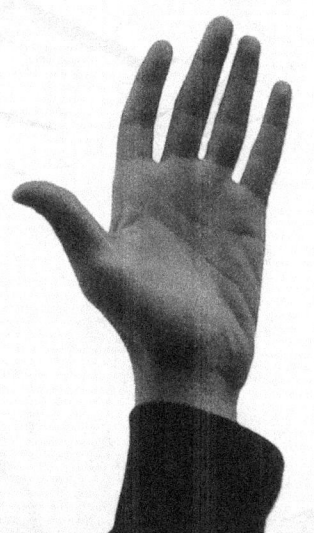

Living Through a Spiritual Pandemic
Joseph A. Conner Sr.

"By Myself I have sworn, declares the Lord, because you have done this thing and have not withheld your son, your only son, indeed I will greatly bless you, and I will greatly multiply your seed as the stars of the heavens and as the sand which is on the seashore;"
Genesis 22:16-17 (NKJV)

The phrase, "in over your head," is part of a group of idioms that have found their way into African American colloquialism. Although they may not be perfect English, they make perfect sense. I'm sure you are familiar with many of them. Some of the expressions you've heard your mother and grandmother say are: 'everything that glitters ain't gold,' 'don't judge a book by its cover,' what you see ain't always what you get,' and the very popular one, 'the grass always looks greener on the other side of the fence.' When one is in over one's head, the suggestion is that you are in a difficult situation that is beyond your understanding and beyond your brain power or area of expertise.

Perhaps, Abraham would have found refuge in these statements. Maybe it would have provided some consultation for those thoughts to be present when God made the request for Abraham to give the life of his son as an offering. Before we examine the text closer, let's examine why God would ask something like this from Abraham in the first place. Why would God consider, even remotely, that Abraham would do such a drastic thing? Let's consider Abraham's faith and obedience.

For a moment, let's deal with Abraham's faith which was a collage of ups and downs. The ups and downs were incurred from the numerous trials and tests that he faced over his lifetime which worked him in ways that expanded his ability to trust God. You must always keep in mind, a believer's walk with God is a walk of faith. Faith can only be matured through the endurance of stressful trials, tribulations, and persecutions. Faith comes by hearing the message of Christ (Romans 10:17), but the developing and maturing process is reserved for hands-on-training.

Faith also requires that works are performed alongside it. James reminds us that faith without works is dead. Our works must be a testimony of what we believe, and what we believe must coincide with what we do. Abraham's faith-building journey with God began when God requested that he leave his familiar surroundings and follow God's instructions. Those instructions brought him into a new dwelling place where his faith development began. Imagine how difficult it must have been to leave the comfort of the familiar. Then, God raised the stakes and requested the unthinkable…kill Isaac!

Kill Isaac? Kill the son of promise! Kill the seed through who nations are supposed to be born? What possible good could emerge from this? When life presents you with these kinds of questions, keep in mind that strong faith is often developed in the tensions of life's challenges. Faith demonstrates itself more fully in the hard places of life. Here, God is stretching Abraham's parental love to the maximum, and he's doing it on a stage of faith. It was on this same stage, a few years earlier, that Abraham, in his old age, had to believe God for Isaac's birth. One must wonder how God really evaluates our faith. What is clear is, even if the evaluation process is cloudy, without faith, it is impossible to please God.

Secondly, let's examine Abraham's walk of obedience which was an extreme one! What kind of man, who was blessed to father a son in the twilight years of his life, would be willing to take the life of that child, on God's command? The task that is set before Abraham is one that will allow God to demonstrate how obedience is better than sacrifice. Man and woman's call to obedience must be attached to their performance.

God had faith in Abraham's ability to trust His wisdom. So, God knew He could count on Abraham's ability to obey Him, regardless of the circumstance. Likewise, Abraham had confidence in God's ability to carry out His promises. Abraham must have had some encounters with God that suggested to him, God would never ask anything of him that ultimately wouldn't turn out for his good.

We are expected to live a life of faith and our faith must progress. Last year's faith can only serve as a catalyst for this year's growth and further faith development. God never tests us in areas that He has not previously prepared us for. Consequently, there had to have been some prior faith encounters to solidify this unusual request from God.

Therefore, we can pray the prayer of Jabez: Oh, that thou would bless me indeed, and enlarge my coast, and that thine hand might be with me, and that thou would keep me from evil, that it may not grieve me! And God granted him that which he requested.

It Was Unexpected!
I Was Not Ready!
June A. Conner

"I lift up my eyes to the mountains—where does my help come from? My help comes from the Lord, the Maker of heaven and earth."
Psalm 121:1-2 (NIV)

It was unexpected! It was unwanted! I told God that I was not ready! After picking my brother up from the nursing home as he recuperated from a stroke with an infected foot, the doctor said in order to work on his foot, he needed to be brought to the emergency room of the hospital so he could monitor the infection. Unfortunately, when I got him to the hospital, they informed me that he had already contracted the COVID-19 virus while at the nursing home. The director of the nursing home had never mentioned that he was sick.

Three days later, his doctor called and told us his body was too weak to fight off the virus. He already had the existing problems of bad lungs and kidneys as well as fighting this serious infection in his foot. His doctor called and asked for a conference call with our family. The doctors, upon examination, had determined that he would never walk out of this hospital alive.

    This news hit me like a ton of bricks. I prayed that this would somehow turn around. *Lord, they have to be wrong* is all I could think. His stroke had only happened a couple of months ago and he had gone to rehab and was doing much better. We were preparing for him to come home. Each day, my younger brother was renovating and fixing up his apartment for his return. He had asked for a new computer, which I purchased, to replace his old one so that he could get online easily as he recovered from his stroke. What did they mean, he would not walk out of this hospital? He had only been there four days. It was exactly eight days from the time I took him to the emergency room to the time we got the call that he was gone.

    What do we do when God has decided to allow something that we are not ready for? Because of COVID-19, we could not visit him in the hospital even though it was only a few blocks from my home. Thank God, there was a compassionate nurse who would call us each morning and allow us to talk to him through Facetime until he was no longer responding. Each day we could see him sinking lower and lower. After receiving one of these calls the day before he died, I knew he was at the end. I couldn't stand it; my heart was breaking. I broke down, and in between sobs told my husband, "This cannot happen…I am not ready for this!" I had never lost a sibling before, and I was not ready to lose one now. "God, this is my big brother" I pleaded, "I need you to heal him!"

Part 1: Lord, I'm Stressed!

Unfortunately, while experiencing my own grief, there were many people who were going through the same thing. I was calling others and trying to give them comfort as my heart was breaking. A friend's father died, another friend's mother succumbed to the virus, and I was calling and praying with them. The question prevails: how do you go forward when you get blindsided by life? What do you do when God in His infinite wisdom moves in a way that leaves you dazed and devastated?

All I knew to do was to try to look around and see who else was going through. I got a call from a young lady who informed me that someone I knew had lost their father. I was able to call and pray with her. When going through, it helps when we stop focusing on ourselves and try to help others. That may sound crazy, but it helps to keep from dwelling on your situation. If you can't do anything about your problem, why not try to help someone else?

The next day, my brother was nonresponsive on the Facetime call, and later that day he passed. I never asked God "why," because I knew from past experiences that it is usually fruitless to ask that question. The only thing that we can do when something like this happens is to crawl up inside the refuge that God provides. That old hymn, "Rock of Ages, cleft for me" kept running through my mind: "Let me hide myself in Thee." Psalm 46 says, "God is my refuge and my strength, a very present help in the time of trouble."

Even though we don't understand, we must trust God enough to believe that God and God alone knows what is best. He has the ability to look down through time and determine what is best for you and your loved ones. Yes, it will hurt. When someone you love passes, it leaves a large hole in your heart. There is a space that nothing else fills. So, the only answer is to ask God to help you accept what He allows.

One young lady that I was ministering to in the loss of her father, asked me if the hurt gets better. Having lost my father in 2007, I was able to tell her that time, with God's help, eventually pushes that hurt to the back burner enough so that we can go on with our lives. It's not gone, but it is not at the forefront of our lives. I'm glad she reminded me of that. Our only alternative is to yield to the will of God and ask God to heal the hurt and give us the strength to stand. We must ask God to wrap us in his cocoon of love as we heal from the hurt of our grief until we can emerge as fully functioning human beings.

Cry. It's a natural thing to do, but don't stay there. When we stop crying, we start putting one foot in front of the other and keep our eyes on God. We can make it if we remember where our help comes from.

GPS
Audrey Moody

"My sheep listen to my voice; I know them, and they follow me."
John 10: 27

I was following my GPS, driving to an unfamiliar destination. It got me there safely, with no problems. When I arrived, I turned off my car and proceeded to the event. I had a great time, enjoyed a delicious meal, and good fellowship. When I got back into my car, I turned on the GPS to lead me home. Leaving the parking lot, I began to realize that the voice of the previous GPS setting was still operating. I was going around in circles—heading back to my original destination.

But I also heard another voice, and I really could not figure out what to do. So around in circles I went. It finally occurred to me that one voice was leading me toward home, and another voice was leading me back to where I had just come from. I pushed buttons, but I was unable to turn off the original directions. I could have stopped and turned the GPS system off and started again. That would have been the wise thing to do, but I continued to drive. I had to determine which voice I was supposed to listen to if I was to get my passengers and myself home. (I did have passengers, but they were so glad not to be driving that they just chatted gleefully with each other as we rode in circles.)

The GPS voices were both soft female voices: low and smooth. One was soft and slow; the other clipped and just a little louder. Both were clear, articulate, pleasant voices. It was difficult to determine which one I was supposed to listen to if we were to get home.

Finally, I was able to determine that the softer, slower voice would direct me right back to the place I had just left. The clipped, louder voice would direct me toward home. All the way down the highway, that soft voice would have me turn around and head back to where I had just come from. If I was to get home, I had to ignore the soft, slow voice and listen to the louder, clipped voice.

That is how it is in life. We hear and even listen to several voices—all of which sound quite alike. The voices are often are hard to distinguish from each other. There are many voices that speak to us: soft slow voices, reassuring, caring sounds, soothing smooth voices that would have us going in the wrong direction, going in circles, going back to those places from which we came, back to the places from which we fought hard to escape. These are voices that lead to confusion and chaos.

We must be clear about the voices we hear—the voices we listen to. How we do that is crucial. Our spiritual disciplines are those things that keep us clear: prayer, reading the Word, reading encouraging books, and listening to and talking to the right people. Our God promises so much as we keep our ears attuned to Him and His Word. God promises perfect peace. God promises His constant presence.

Say this prayer:

Dear God, we are your people, and we thank You for loving us enough to give clarity to your Word and your will. Help us to listen carefully for your voice. Even in times of confusion and chaos, You speak. Give us ears to hear You and faith to obey You.

A Sound Mind!
June A. Conner

"For God hath not given us the spirit of fear; but of power, and of love, and of a sound mind."
2 Timothy 1:7 (KJV)

There are two things you don't want to hear from your doctor when you are suffering extreme pain. The first is, "I am sorry, but after extensive tests, we don't know what is causing your pain." Month after month, test after test came back negative for any illness or disease. My doctor apologized that she couldn't tell me what was causing this pain. "The only thing that seems to be abnormal is your sed rate; it seems to be a little high," she said. Of course, I asked what was a sed rate.

Sed rate is short for sedimentation rate and is a number in our body that tells the doctor when something is wrong. If it is high, there is inflammation in your body. My thought was that I certainly didn't need a sed rate to tell that something was wrong. I was in excruciating, burning pain that started at the top of my head and traveled down my body causing my muscles to tighten and me to scream in pain. I needed to know what this was so that it could be fixed ASAP!

Oh Lord, Why Me?

The second thing you don't want to hear from your doctor is, "We finally know what is causing your pain, but there is no cure." The only thing we can do is try to treat it, but you will have to be in treatment for the rest of your life, and it manifests differently for each person." The words kept ringing in my head. There is no cure! That is how I was told that I had Multiple Sclerosis.

How do we handle it when we are given a devastating diagnosis? How do we as Christians even begin to deal with the news, be it lupus, cancer, or any number of conditions that we know entail a long, painful fight? I must tell you that all of the great scriptures of the Bible don't come to you immediately, at least they didn't come to me. My thoughts swirled: *What will become of my two young children?* They were one year and five-years-old, respectively. Would I be able to care for them? Would I be able to continue my job? Working each day as a schoolteacher is a very demanding job. Teaching was one of the things I enjoyed. Yes, I had a working husband, but our finances were built on two salaries. Would I wind up needing someone to take care of me or have to reside in a nursing home? *God, what did I do to deserve this? Oh Lord, why me?*

We often begin to tremble at what the future might hold for us, and out of that fear we panic. Like Job in chapter 7:11, when he says that he can no longer restrain his mouth and needed to speak out in the anguish of his spirit and the bitterness of his soul. I, too, began to speak out of the anguish of my spirit and complain in the bitterness of my soul.

Part 1: Lord, I'm Stressed!

This fear caused me to project into a dismal future and see a grim picture of what my life would be like.

Whenever I went to my neurologist office, I saw people blind and lame—in wheelchairs and on walkers—and it caused me to be frightened and unsettled. I woke up each day wondering what would finally happen to me. This continued until one day coming from my doctor's visit, I decided to stop at a spot along West River Drive where you could see the water through the trees and overgrown brush. It had always had a calming effect on me and this particular day, the sun was shining, and a light breeze was blowing.

While sitting there and pouring my heart out to God, the Spirit gave me this scripture, "For God has not given us the spirit of fear, but of love, and of power and of a sound mind" (2 Tim 1:7). As a child of God, the realization struck me that whatever was going to happen was already in God's hands. Just as I had been taught all of my life to have faith that God was guiding my life, I realized that panic was not necessary because whatever happened, I would not have to face it alone. Constantly projecting, "What if," would only raise my stress levels and make my situation worse. The question, "Oh Lord, why me?," just added to that stress. I could not give in to fear!

I had to believe that God already had it worked out for my good. At the age of 37, I would have to lean on those Sunday school lessons and sermons on faith that I had heard over the years. The old songs of the church that my mother constantly sang such as "Leaning on the Everlasting Arms" and "What a Friend We have in Jesus," would be some of the songs that calmed my spiraling mind.

> "What a fellowship, what a joy divine
> Leaning on the everlasting arms
> What a blessedness, what a peace is mine
> Leaning on the everlasting arms"

> "What a friend we have in Jesus,
> all our sins and griefs to bear!
> What a privilege to carry
> everything to God in prayer."

When you get hit with something unexpected, remember that God is and always will be with you. Whenever I start to go to that dark place of fear and doubt, I remind myself that fear is our enemy. It keeps us from relying on God and concentrating on His grace. It's been thirty years or more since that time, and I have to tell you that God has been with me every step of the way. God's grace and mercy have given me the strength to work until retirement, raise my children with my husband to adulthood, while singing, teaching, and preaching God's word. How? Because God has not given me a spirit of fear, but the courage of a sound mind to continue on with Him by my side!

PART TWO:
Lord, I'm Weary!

"If we want to be reconciled to God, we have to suffer sometimes. If we want the sunshine, we have to go through a little rain."

JAC

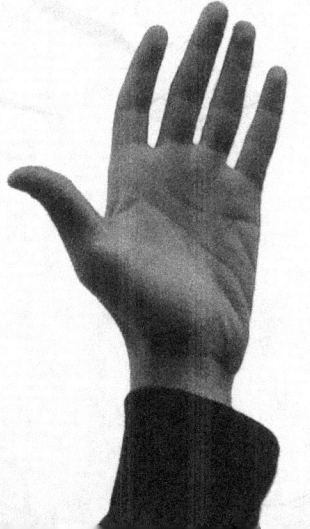

I'm Tired of Being Tired
Joseph A. Conner

And you will seek Me and find Me, when you search for Me with all your heart. I will be found by you, says the LORD, and I will bring you back from your captivity; I will gather you from all the nations and from all the places where I have driven you, says the Lord, and I will bring you to the place from which I cause you to be carried away captive.
Jeremiah 29:13-14 (NKJV)

Couched in the context of the first Jewish deportation to Babylon, the word in this text is for both Israel and for us. God had declared that the time would come when 'exile' for Israel would not be a choice but rather an 'existential reality.' No longer would they be at ease in Jerusalem, but according to God's plan, they would pay for their unfaithfulness. As the prophets before Jeremiah had already prophesied, Israel did indeed go into near slavery. And now, having been in captivity for only a short while, they were weary, confused, and bewildered.

Could it be that every now and then you and I also need this unique opportunity for a "Babylonian experience" in which God coddles us in a crucible of correction, takes us to the potter's house and works a work on us with the potter's wheel, breaks us, and makes us into new vessels? This word for the weary comes with two aspects of its own power and validity. Jeremiah offers a word that has both purpose and promise.

The purpose of this captivity was clear. For years, Israel had sought her own; her priests and prophets had gone astray and the hearts of the children had been turned from the fathers. The proverbial saying that "the fathers had eaten bitter grapes, setting the children's teeth on edge" had become a reality. God would not deliver Israel from that which she needed to experience. Some time in captivity was a given. Little did Israel know that no matter how others tried to define what God was doing, God's plan for her was wrapped up in Kairos time, which could not be merely counted or measured by chronological exactness, but rather by Israel's willingness to seek God with her whole heart.

Jeremiah's word of purpose was forget what Zedekiah, Hananiah, and the others have said about checking out early. You are going to be in Babylon for a while. Don't let them fill your heads with dreams of a speedy return to Jerusalem. They are not sent from the Lord but are instruments of their own imaginations. Go ahead, build some houses, and settle down. Plant gardens from which to eat and feed your families. Make sure that your sons and daughters are marrying and bearing children so that your heritage might remain. Seek the peace and prosperity of the city to which you have gone. Pray for it, because if you want your own deliverance, you've got to concentrate on helping someone else. God is going to use you, even in captivity.

In our own lives, Babylon will occur. There will be times when our estrangement from God will lead us to places of spiritual soul searching and pondering. For us, Babylon is not a place, but rather an experience or quality of existence that defines our relationship with God. We have to go to Babylon. There is no shortcut to our commitment, no stops along the way for our spiritual stamina, or no fumbling around with our faith. This is serious business! We must go to Babylon!

There will always be those who prefer the shortcut to faithfulness. There are those who would convince you that this is not God's plan for you, that you can have peace and prosperity without going through all the discomfort and uneasiness that you may be experiencing in your "Babylonian journey." But if we really want to appreciate Jerusalem and get back home spiritually, we must go to Babylon.

Stay in Babylon. I'm convinced that God has an upside-down theology! If we want to be reconciled to God, we have to suffer sometimes. If we want the sunshine, we have to go through a little rain. If we want to be strong, we have to go to some weakening places. If we want to get closer, we have to experience some estrangement. If we want to rejoice, we have to shed a few tears. Stay in Babylon!

This word for the weary was not only a word that signifies God's purpose for our lives, but it is a powerful word of promise. Listen to the Word of God from the lips of Jeremiah in Jeremiah 29:10-14:

> "For thus says the LORD: After seventy years are completed at Babylon, I will visit you and perform My good word toward you, and cause you to return to this place. For I know the thoughts that I think toward you, says the Lord, thoughts of peace and not of evil, to give you a future and a hope. Then you will call upon Me and go and pray to Me, and I will listen to you. And you will seek Me and find *Me*, when you search for Me with all your heart. I will be found by you, says the Lord, and I will bring you back from your captivity; I will gather you from all the nations and from all the places where I have driven you, says the Lord, and I will bring you to the place from which I cause you to be carried away captive."

These beautiful and poetic words of promise remind Israel that God has not forgotten and never will forget her. For after her time had been accomplished, the promise of restoration was sure. What a word for some weary exiles! What a word for some tired children of God! What a word for those sinking in the lowlands of languishing! What a word for those drowning in the depths of despair!

What a word of promise! In God's own time, He grants that the sufferings of this present time are consumed with the joy of knowing that He never forsakes his own. You and I have the blessed assurance in knowing that all things work according to the plan of the eternal and that no matter what we are going through, we need only remember

Part 2: Lord, I'm Weary!

that God has not forgotten us. The battle is not ours; it's the Lord's. We can't afford to forfeit what God has for us by leaving Babylon too soon, for only after seventy years can we experience the blessings of the "then" existence. We have to wait until the weariness of our existence finds hope in the prophetic "then." We can live in Babylon as long as there is a "then." What a word for the weary!

This message to the exiles reminds us that God never leaves us without hope. In the midst of our alienation, God always comes to us. Jeremiah's "then" leaped over some forty and two generations and got wrapped up in a "now." Now God has come to us in person, a word in the flesh, a word for us weary travelers. Now God has come to us through the sacrificial death of Jesus on a rugged cross called Calvary and a hill called Golgotha. God has made good on a promise of restoration. In Jesus, God killed death on the cross and allowed your Lord and mine to rise up with all power in His hands. Now God says, "I know the plans I have for you. You have a future and a hope. When you call me, I will answer. When you seek me and pray to me, I will hear you. When you seek me with your whole heart, I will be found of you. Now, God says, "there is a place I've prepared for you. It's the camp land in New Jerusalem. So, walk together, children, don't you get weary. Sing together, children, don't you get weary. Pray together children, don't you get weary in Babylon. There's a great camp meeting in the Promised Land."

This is Not the Time
Marsha Brown Woodard

"Let's not be weary in doing good, for we will reap in due season, if we don't give up."
Galatians 6:9 WEB *(World English Bible)*

Even if you feel like giving up, this is not the time to stop working for justice. This is not the time for those who have been working to tear down systems of oppression to give up. Even when it appears that change is slow in coming, this is not the time to stop. Even when it seems that each day brings the news of another tragedy, it still is not the time to turn in the towel nor throw up your hands in disgust.

Even as I write these words, I can hear the reader say, "But you don't know my situation. You have no idea how much I have tried, how many meetings I have sat through, or how much defeat I have experienced. You don't know how tired I really am." And my response would be yes, you are tired, yes you have tried over and over again. Yes, you have sat through more meetings than you can count, but even so, this is not the time to stop!

In our humanness, we want to see an answer, we want to experience success, and we want change to come, but that is not always how God works. In Galatians 6:9, we are reminded that we should not get weary in doing what is good. Working for justice is a good thing. Working to dismantle systems of injustice is a good thing. This is the kind of work that God calls His people to do, but in the midst of doing the work, we sometimes get tired. I was reminded that God sometimes takes a long time to manifest the change we are expecting. Even though God could change situations in the twinkling of an eye, sometimes God chooses to work through humans.

One place this is seen is in the Old Testament when God brings the Israelites out of bondage from Egypt. The children of Israel had been enslaved for 400 years and things appeared to get worse instead of better. There were generations who died believing freedom would come, but they never saw it. I believe that when we look closely, we see God working through the people to bring them to freedom. We see Shiphrah and Puah, the Hebrew midwives who refused to kill the male babies on the birthing stool, and thereby outwitted and outmaneuvered Pharaoh. Later, we will see Jochebed, Moses' mother, hiding him as long as she could and then trusting God as she placed him on the water. We discover that even Pharaoh's daughter became part of God's process when the baby Moses is found. She provided resources for his mother to raise him, and later he lived in the palace with her. God even uses intangible things like bushes that don't burn as part of the process.

While Moses was away, Miriam and Aaron have been working in the community, and at just the right moment, God sends Moses back to Egypt. But Moses cannot do the work alone; it required the elders, Miriam, Aaron, and everyone working together to gain their freedom. If any of the pieces had been missing, it may have prevented the very freedom they desired. That is why this is not the time for us to stop working for justice.

In our time, we often look around and wonder how long before everyone will be treated with respect and dignity. How long will there be a need for marches? When will there be enough laws on the books so that freedom is not a dream but a reality? How long, how long? And while I can't say how long it will be, I can say that we cannot stop no matter how tired we might be. We are the fruit of others' dreams. Previous generations prayed for the things we take for granted. Women and men gave their lives for the freedom we now experience. So now we must continue to work even in the midst of our tiredness.

This is not the time to stop, but it is time for everyone to join in the work. We need women and men, boys and girls, old and young, rich and poor, to find the work they can do and then do it with all their might. We need letters written and phone calls made. We need marches and demonstrations. We need articles and books written. We need coalitions developed. We need educators to teach the next generation. We need preachers to proclaim the power of a liberating Gospel. We need you to not be weary in well doing but recommit yourself to the task at hand. You can't be weary because there are laws that need to be changed and there are systems of injustice that need to be dismantled. At every level, there is work waiting to be done.

So, in this time, there will be days when you feel the pain, and days when you weep, moan and cry, but because you believe in freedom, this is not the time to give up, but instead, this is the time to continue the work even in the midst of your tears. This is the time to remember that we stand on the shoulders of women and men who gave their lives for the work of freedom.

This is the time to remember that we, like the Israelites and our ancestors, may not see the fulfillment of the vision, but that is okay, for God only calls us to be faithful in our season even as they were faithful in theirs. This is the time to hold on and not be weary in the work of freedom and justice.

Say this prayer:

Dear God, grant us the courage to continue the work even on the days when we are tired and weary. Help us, God, not give up but to be faithful to our assignment. Help us remember that you are always with us. Amen.

Life Happens!
June A. Conner

"What, then, shall we say in response to these things? If God is for us, who can be against us? He who did not spare his own Son, but gave him up for us all—how will he not also, along with him, graciously give us all things?"
Romans 8:31-32 (NIV)

Have you ever gone through a situation where no matter how you prayed, it just didn't seem to get better? When you went to sleep you woke up with the same stresses and problems from the day before. You are saved and have faith that God is with you, but the same daily mental or physical challenges confront you day after day. You don't want to give up and you want to continue to stand on God's promises, but your mind and spirit are stressed and tired and it seems as though situations are staying the same no matter what you do.

I sat in church and listened to a sermon that overall, I thought was a good word, but it left me with questions. I guess a good sermon is supposed to make you think. The preacher told us that whatever you are going through as a child of God, don't despair, because whatever we are going through will get better. He told us not to give up and to realize that we are guaranteed through the Word of God that things are going to work out for our good. Of course, he based it on the scripture, "And we know that in all things God works for the good of those who love him, who have been called according to his purpose" (Romans 8:28) and," If God is for us, who can be against us?" (Romans 8:31b)

Admittedly, I believe this, but because of the aggravating and exasperating situation that I was enduring, I had to ask the questions, "What are we supposed to do until then?" and "What do we do until it gets better?"

Sometimes life balls up its fist and hits you in the stomach. Not a light tap that you just shrug off, but one of those punches that make you double over in pain, and knocks the wind out of you. It's one of those punches that leave you lightheaded and dazed. As a child, I used to love Saturday afternoons because sometimes I was allowed to watch boxing with my father. It amazed me the kind of punishment that the human body could take. Most of the time, the boxers would get hit over and over and just shake it off and keep punching. But sometimes I would watch one boxer bring his fist back and swing forward with such force that it would leave his opponent staggering and dazed often right before he hit the mat. He was not always out, but he was definitely dazed and down, at least for a few seconds.

If it was a boxer that we liked, I would start yelling, Get up, get up!" My father never yelled; he was a quiet man, but he would motion for the man to get up. Suddenly there would be a cheer as the boxer staggered to his feet for the continued round of the boxing match. Life is sometimes like that.

We can be going along in our lives, pursuing our jobs, attending church, and spending time with our families, and all of a sudden, something comes out of the blue to rock our world. It can be the job that has been so secure is suddenly in jeopardy. It can be the relationship that seemed so steady and so nurturing goes sideways for some inexplicable reason. You break up with the love of your life or worse still, your spouse cheats on you. It can be the child that you were most proud of for being so steady and responsible does something so wrong and out of character that you can't believe it, or worse yet, ends up on drugs or some other addiction! It leaves you wondering, what in the world happened. Life happened!

So, as we are getting battered about, what do we do? We have been told that God is coming, and that God will deliver, but the preacher never said *when* God is coming! So, I ask again, what do we do? We wait. Yes, we wait. But we do not wait sitting still and getting beat and buffeted. We do not wait angry and depressed. We wait in prayer, asking God to give us the next direction of where we are to go and what we should do. We wait, putting one foot in front of the other with spirit-driven strength knowing that no matter how bad it looks, God still has our lives firmly in hand. As Jeremiah tells us, God has a plan for our lives. We trust in that plan and we wait in faith. Dictionary.com[1] says that *faith* is trust in a person or thing. Our trust is in God, and we exercise this faith by waiting on Him. Job says, "All the days of my appointed time will I wait, till my change comes" (Job 14:14 KJV).   We wait for our change to come by shielding ourselves with the comforting scriptures that let us know that God is our refuge and our strength, a very present help in the time of trouble. Our faith helps us believe that God has already dispatched an angel to fight our battle who may be taking a little longer because they are getting through the traffic jam that Satan has thrown up to keep us tied up in knots. But we still wait, because we are more than conquerors through Jesus Christ.

    Children of God, we wait with a positive and believing mind that help is on the way and that God in God's almighty wisdom, knows what God is doing and has never been late. We wait, knowing that it gets better no matter who is against us because God is still for us. We wait with a faith that lets us believe that though we cannot see it coming, we know deliverance is on the way.

[1] www.dictionary.com. Faith, accessed June 29, 2020

I Can't Breathe
Joseph A. Conner Sr.

"Be merciful to me, O God, be merciful to me for my soul trusts in You; And in the shadow of Your wings I will make my refuge, Until these calamities have passed by."
Psalm 57:1 (NKJV)

The most spiritual person in the world faces crises—turning points of sudden, unpredictable, and unexpected occurrences. What makes something a crisis is the fact that we have no apparent control over the situation. I am talking about crises that we do not bring upon ourselves, for some of us are going through things that are the result of our own doing. Since we sowed bad seeds, now we must find a way to undo a bad harvest or find a way to live through it. Here, I am talking about times when we find ourselves faced with a situation in which we do not know how to proceed.

Things happen even to the saints, even to the best of us, with all of our faith, all of our power from the Holy Spirit, and all of our shouting and praising God. Even with all of these things we cannot stop crises from coming into our lives.

We may as well admit it—things fall apart.

We may as well admit it—things come loose.

We may as well admit it—things break down, and crises come even in our spiritual lives.

We have to climb some mountains in our Christian walk, and sometimes, it is the rough side of the mountain that we must climb. Sometimes, it is a hard climb with no trolley car to take us to the top, and at other times, it is a hard slide back into the valley. Life is not all mountaintops or valleys, but a mixture.

We are not going to be crisis free.

We are not going to be burden free.

We are not going to be trial free.

We have to do more than cry our way through life. We need to know how to handle a crisis situation without panicking and making things worse. I found the key in Psalm 57.

David found help in Psalm 57:1. He writes, "Be merciful unto me, O God, be merciful unto me for my soul thirsteth: yea, in the shadow of thy wings will I make my refuge, until these calamities be over-past.

Your Discontent came to pass.

Your Indebtedness came to pass.

Your Distress came to pass.

In other words, it did not come to last. When the pastor is not around, when the deacons, missionaries, and other saints are not around, there are certain things you must know to get through a crisis. First, you have to know it is going to pass. It is not going to last…It came only to pass. Trouble does not last forever if you are a child of God. It does come to an end.

Part 2: Lord, I'm Weary!

In the first verse of Psalm 57—a contemplation of David when he fled from Saul in the cave —David said he would take refuge "in the shadow" of God's wings "until these calamities be over-past." Over-past means passed over or done with. Have mercy on me, God, until these calamities have passed over me.

Cover me until these calamities have passed over me. Stand by me until these calamities have passed over me.

The storm is passing over you, and you must know that God did not bring you this far to leave you. This, too, shall pass.

David said, "Not only am I going to know that this came to pass, but I am going to remember the Source of all my help in previous crises."

PART THREE:
Lord, I Need Your Power!

"Our relationship with God can become synchronized. It requires spending time with Him and learning to be sensitive to the Holy Spirit."

JAC

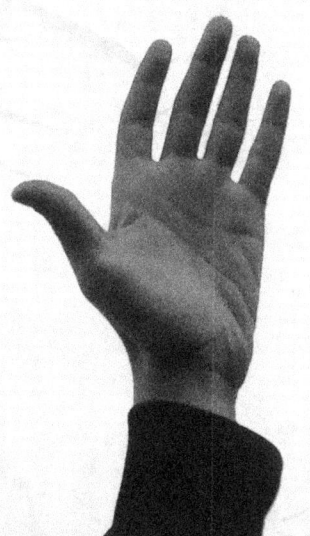

Deliverance from Disappointment
Joseph A. Conner Sr.

"But he gives us more grace. That is why Scripture says: 'God opposes the proud but shows favor to the humble.' Submit yourselves, then, to God. Resist the devil, and he will flee from you. Come near to God and he will come near to you."
James 4:6-8 (NRSV)

Three days? I repeated, wondering what I would do without my car for that long. A neighborhood body shop had fixed a bent tire rim, but the car still wasn't driving right. So, I had brought it back to the dealership for what was turning out to be more extensive service.

"Yes Sir, it'll take that long," the mechanic said. "That pothole you hit did some major damage to your car. We have to order a part from the manufacturer, and it needs a complete realignment."

By taking a shortcut and trying to get by with a "quick fix," I had placed my car in jeopardy. The entire balance system was off. Out of whack. It needed special attention and parts that only the manufacturer could supply. Otherwise, my car would be off the road for good.

Our lives can also get out of whack. We are mind, body and spirit, and unless all three are functioning in balance, we can't operate properly. We need the touch of our Maker and Manufacturer to put us back in alignment. For maximum performance, we need periodic checkups and a regular maintenance plan.

When I left my car that day, the dealership provided me with a loaner, a replacement car to drive until the mechanics finished the repairs on mine. But in life, we can't get a loaner. We must take care of the original body God gave us.

The Bible says that the body is the temple of the Holy Spirit:

"Do you not know that your body is the temple of the Holy Spirit who is in you, whom you have from God, and you are not your own? For you were brought at a price; therefore, glorify God in your body and in your spirit, which are Gods" (1 Corinthians. 6:19-20).

How precious it is to think that the Holy Spirit honors us with His presence. But our "temple" must be able to receive and respect the gift.

Too many people are running around the city, dashing across the nation, or jetting about the world, completely out of sync. It is more than jet lag they are experiencing; it is a spirit lag. They have tried shortcuts and quick fixes—perhaps a drink, a companion, a day off, a mini-vacation here and there—but what they need is to be realigned with God.

When we travel nationally and internationally, we reset our watches as we cross from one time zone into another. I believe there are spiritual time zones as well as physical ones. In the spirit realm, we also cross over from one zone to another—from the old life to the new. Crossing that spiritual zone necessitates an adjustment. It requires getting in step with the Holy Spirit. "Since we live by the Spirit," Paul wrote, "let us keep in step with the Spirit" (Galatians. 5:25).

Keeping in step with the Spirit means synchronizing our spirits with God's Spirit. Have you ever seen the synchronized swimmers in the Olympics? They move with amazing precision, but they do it so gracefully that the synchronization appears almost effortless. That precision, however, is the result of spending hours upon hours practicing as a team and getting the feel for the routine until every swimmer knows each motion intuitively and instinctively.

Our relationship with God can become synchronized. It requires spending time with Him and learning to be sensitive to the Holy Spirit. The Word says, "In him, we live and move and have our being" (Acts 17:28). When we begin to move in sync with God, we will not experience so much stress because our bodies and spirits will be in the same place at the same time, and they will be in step with the Spirit.

When that happens, we will learn how to be content no matter what the circumstances. That was the lesson the apostle Paul learned. He wrote, "I have learned to be content whatever the circumstances. I know what it is to be in need, and I know what it is to have plenty. I have learned the secret of being content in any and every situation, whether well fed or hungry, whether living in plenty or in want" (Philippians 4:11-12).

Paul was content because he was in step with the Spirit. A wonderful, liberating freedom comes when you reach that state of contentment in Christ. That's the point where you realize that stress does not have to stress you out. Situations and circumstances—bad or good—can change. But God is the same yesterday, today, and forever. Get in sync with Him. Learn to be content. You don't have to live on an emotional roller coaster. You can find stability and security, fulfillment and contentment, and perfect peace of mind in Christ. Don't block your blessing: get out of God's way!

Don't Block Your Blessing!

1. Get in sync with God by spending time with Him.
2. Be specific in your prayer requests. Get out of God's way. Submit yourself therefore to God…Resist the devil…

Draw near to God….

Cleanse your hands…purify your hearts…

Humble yourself before the Lord, and He will exalt you.

Don't Panic—Pray. (If my people…)

Don't be Anxious—Rest in God's Assurance. (Cast all your cares…)

In Crisis—Be Confident. (All things work together…)

Feeling Helpless—Keep Hope Alive. (Hope thou in God…)

Feeling Lonely—Lean on the Lord. (Yea though I walk…)

Part 3: Lord, I Need Your Power!

Don't Panic—Praise Him. (I will bless the Lord…)

In Trials—Trust Him. (Come unto me…)

God is Present in the Storm!
Patricia A. Blount

"God is our refuge and strength, a very present help in trouble."
Psalms 46:1

8416 Lyons Place was at that time the residence of my dream home. My husband and I leased the property with a 2-year lease-purchase option, locking in the sale price at $70,000.00. In August of 1987, we moved our family in our new home: a 3-bedroom loft-style townhouse, 1 1/2 baths, laundry area conveniently located on the second floor adjacent to the bedrooms, manicured front lawn, parking garage with an extended driveway, and an enclosed backyard for family enjoyment.

    To finance the purchase, my husband and I opened an additional bank account for the main purpose of setting aside savings toward the settlement costs. Admittedly, my husband was the primary contributor for deposits made to the account, and I assumed more of the household expenses. Seemingly, all was going well, and my dream of purchasing the home was materializing.

    We were now well into this process and with only a few months of the purchase option remaining. At the direction of my husband, I called the realtor to set up an appointment to discuss the details of the purchase. This is where I should have sensed a problem brewing, but I brushed it off. As the talks progressed, I noticed my husband began to point out areas of repairs that needed to be addressed before "putting out any money," which to his credit were legitimate but not deal breakers. We were assured any repairs needed would be handled or with work repair estimates, the costs deducted from the selling price; however, the hedging continued. One complaint began to lead to another in his discussions with me. Unfortunately, at the time, I didn't get it. I didn't get that a storm was brewing.

While running errands one afternoon, I was short a few dollars to pay for a purchase. I made a stop at the ATM to get the cash needed. This is where my dream shattered. Looking at the receipt of the transaction left me horrified! The account balance revealed the secret, and I understood what the hedging and complaining were all about. All except $5000 was gone from the account! This hit me like a storm, and the bottom dropped out of my dream. What do you do when you lose your dream?

Shocked, I almost fainted on the street! Confused and sick to the stomach, reality set in realizing all hopes for this dream was lost. I didn't know the "what" or the "why" this could this happen. I had no idea, but the questions were about to get answered. With only four months remaining of the two-year agreement, it was totally impossible to replace thousands of dollars plus come up with the remaining

Part 3: Lord, I Need Your Power!

funds needed. This *certainly* was an unexpected storm; one I could not fathom, and it took me by surprise. A storm doesn't always announce itself; sometimes the wind just suddenly blows it in, but God is present in the storm!

Already experiencing a seriously bad day, I knew the evening wasn't going to make it any better. With high anxiety, I waited for my husband's arrival home. To say the least, a highly emotional confrontation took place, and to just give you the bottom line, his answer: "It was *My* money." Tell me, what do you do with that?

I found myself standing at one of the windows in my bedroom late one night looking out at the community I had come to love. The night was so peaceful and quiet, contrary to every emotion I was feeling on the inside; feelings of hurt, abandonment, embarrassment, and dread. I was totally devastated; yes, about losing the house, but more importantly, how can a man who claims to love us, do this to us?

Standing there that night I experienced a feeling of hopelessness like I've never felt. I had never understood why a person would want to commit suicide, but for the first time in my life, I understood. I came to understand that a person can experience such a degree of hurt, loss, and devastation that can bring them to the point to contemplate committing such a destructive act; to give up and throw in the towel on life rather than go on living. That night I understood perfectly well how you can lose yourself when finding yourself in a seemingly hopeless situation.

I had faced many difficult challenges in life but nothing I experienced compared to this. While standing at that window I heard myself saying, "God, I'd rather die than go through this."

I knew the pain of that devastation was more than I alone could bear. Something else I knew, and also felt quite strongly, was that I was on the edge of a mental breakdown, but I cried out to God; and I want you to know that God kept me! He was present in my storm. *God is my refuge and strength!* Hallelujah!

I lost that home, but God didn't leave me homeless. In God's faithfulness, He provided another home for me and the children. It was not my dream house, but the home God so graciously provided was a large 3-bedroom home conveniently located across from a park. The children loved it and were excited to move there! I believe God used the children's excitement to settle my emotions and comfort me. Thankfully, I accepted His blessing. There, my inner healing began, and I learned another amazing thing about my Father God; *He is a very present help in trouble!*

Psalms 46 is a wonderful reminder of the care and faithfulness of a loving God to His children. As children of God, we can have full confidence in our Father's protection to be a "refuge" for us and give us "strength" to sustain us in any storm.

In life, we encounter many types of storms, problems, and situations, and no two storms are alike. Some storms are more disastrous in their destructive paths than others, but that is the nature of a storm. But know, God is our refuge and strength, a very present help in trouble, because God is present in the storm.

Watch Out!
Audrey E. Moody

"Further, my brothers and sisters, rejoice in the Lord! It is no trouble for me to write the same things to you again, and it is a safeguard for you. Watch out for those dogs, those evildoers, those mutilators of the flesh."
Philippians 3:1-2 (NIV)

The men walked into the room in a quiet and orderly way. They were neat; some clean shaven, some bearded, some with kufis. All were dressed in dark blue sweatpants and light blue cotton tops. All of them had bracelets on their right wrists. We were seated at long blue tables on hard orange plastic chairs. This was not a church service, high school graduation, or a college commencement. We were in a stark visiting room. It was a prison. It was the graduation ceremony from a program whose goal was to enable incarcerated men never to return to prison again. They had already been seduced by "the dogs, the evil doers, and the mutilators of the flesh." They had succumbed to the wiles of the streets, the lure of drugs, and the enticement of fast money. Their crimes were often petty misdemeanors, perhaps a rare, major felony.

Our presence among them was to celebrate a milestone with them. The men who spoke were articulate and passionate as they described their learning experiences, praised and thanked their teachers and mentors, and repeated their mantras and pledges. They spoke about their determination not to return to prison. They thanked their families for not giving up on them. We gave words of encouragement; we told them that there is a better way to guide their lives, We also told them that we had their backs and prayed for their futures. I wonder, though, how often do we, the church, really support those men and women who have been incarcerated and who return to our communities looking for another chance.

How well do we recognize and celebrate the gifts God has given them? But more importantly, perhaps, how well do we recognize and challenge the systems that converge to place men and women in the way of the "mutilators of the flesh?" How well do we recognize and challenge educational systems that target our young men as early as the fourth grade for failure? How well do we recognize and challenge those prison systems that are built in the rural parts of our states, waiting for our young men? How well do we recognize and challenge those health care systems that deny our young men easy access? How often do we, the church, hear clearly what the prophet Micah speaks as the oracle from the heart and mind of God: "What does the Lord require of you? To do justice, to love mercy, to walk humbly..." How often do we act?'

Part 3: Lord, I Need Your Power!

Say this prayer:

God, we thank You for those men and women who have lost their way and whom You have placed in our lives. Enable us to demonstrate your provision of safety and protection from the dogs and evildoers and mutilators of the flesh. Empower us to love mercy and walk humbly....and do justice. Amen

Waiting for Morning!
June A. Conner

"Because of the Lord's great love, we are not consumed, for his compassions never fail. They are new every morning; great is your faithfulness."
Lamentations 3:22-23 (NIV)

While walking through the hospital during visitation, I had the opportunity to speak to a mother who was sitting vigilantly beside the bed of her seriously ill son. Her son, a formerly healthy teenage young man, had suddenly become ill to the point of hospitalization. This poor mother couldn't figure out why her healthy son was lying in a hospital bed instead of being in school or out with his friends.

Upon entering their room, I noticed that she was seated on a large-cushioned bench that the hospital had in the rooms so that parents could stay by the bed of their sick child. There was a large window behind her where the sun was streaming in, and her son was asleep in the bed in front of her.

I asked how he was doing, and she looked up at me, smiled, and said, "Much better than last week." I then asked her what had changed because her son was still hooked up to several machines with tubes running everywhere.

    She stated that last week, the doctor came into the hospital room to tell her that her child's condition had worsened and that they were not sure of the outcome of his treatment. The only thing they could do now was to wait and see if it worked. This mother, shaken, had asked the doctor what could be done while they waited. "Nothing," the doctor replied. "If he makes it through tonight, he has a chance of recovery."

    Having two children of my own, it was hard to imagine getting the news that my child was that close to death. Being a woman of faith, she informed me that she had called her family and those prayer warriors she knew to inform them of the doctor's words and solicited their prayers. She then sat on the couch in his room determined to spiritually fight for his life. She said, "I sat on that couch and stared up at the night sky and talked to God praying as I waited through the night; I couldn't go to sleep," she said. Her fear was that if she did, he wouldn't make it. Her response was: "I sat here because I was **waiting for morning**."

    "It was a long night, but when the light from the early morning sunrise began to come through the window, and my child was still alive, I began to thank and praise God." She said, "So, Sis. June, anything after that night is a bonus!" I asked her if it was okay to tell her story and she said definitely! Her child kept improving until he was able to walk out of that hospital a few weeks later.

Part 3: Lord, I Need Your Power!

My thoughts were what a great lesson for us to learn. When night comes and things look darkest, sometimes we have to hunker down, gather the prayer warriors, and do spiritual warfare as we wait for morning. The scripture tells us that, "Weeping may endure for a night, but joy cometh in the morning" (Ps.30:5b). We remember in the Bible when Paul and Silas were shackled in jail, they prayed and sang songs all night. Their future looked dark, but they did not stop singing and praying until the shackles fell off. I believe they prayed and sang because they knew that God had not forgotten them. Despite what the circumstances looked like, despite what their bodies were feeling, and despite what their future might hold, they knew that God was still with them; that God had not forgotten them, and that they still had an advocate with God.

How many of you have ever been or are now in a dark situation not knowing which way it is going to resolve itself, not knowing what direction you should go in, and understanding that whatever is going to happen is completely out of your control? Whatever dark night you are experiencing, know that it will not last always. We have to believe that morning is coming if we pray, keep the faith, and just hold on.

PART FOUR:
Lord, I Need Your Help!

"Our God promises so much as we keep our ears attuned to Him and His Word. God promises perfect peace. God promises His constant presence."

Audrey E. Moody

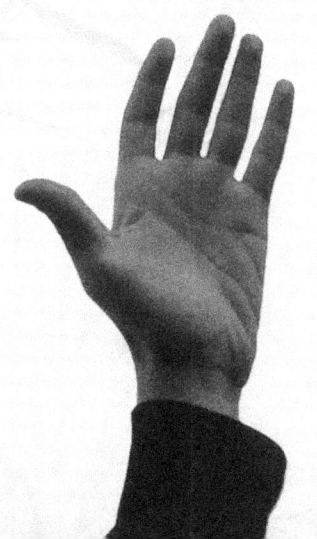

Handling Life's Detours
Joseph A. Conner Sr.

"Then the manna ceased on the day after they had eaten the produce of the land; and the children of Israel no longer had manna, but they ate the food of the land of Canaan that year."
Joshua 5:12 (NKJV)

Manna was the bread provided directly by God's divine power for the children of Israel after their exodus from Egypt. In our text, it appears at first glance that God had ceased to provide food for his people: "And the manna ceased on the morrow after they had eaten of the old corn of the land" (Joshua 5:12). But then the text goes on to say, "No manna appeared that day, and it was never seen again. So, from that time on, the Israelites ate from the crops of Canaan" (5:12). From all accounts, the manna had been significantly replaced with corn.

Once in the Promised Land, the manna ceased, and the Israelites were to eat of the fruit of the land of Canaan. Their new staple, corn, involved greater and more continuous labor than taking a container and gathering what had fallen from heaven. This was not an issue for the first year because they could eat the corn that had been left behind by the Canaanites, but eventually, they would have to work for their food. While the corn was still the provision of God, the children of Israel would now have to take personal responsibility for growing it. God upped the ante; it was time for them to grow up. The new land called for a new way of surviving. God had substituted the miracle of the manna with something different but equally as marvelous.

There are several important lessons to be learned from this text. First, there will be times when we have to live our lives under drastically changed conditions. Sometimes the change is for the better. It may be a job with great potential for advancement, generous pay, and excellent benefits. It may be an inheritance that brightens our financial situations. Perhaps we will meet and marry our helpmate, leading to a new home, security, and happiness.

There are also times when things change for the worse. We may experience seasons when the manna appears to have ceased when the things we are accustomed to receiving with little or no effort are no longer available. It may be losing the health plan that was a part of our employment package and now we're faced with paying for our own medical insurance or going without and praying that no one in our families becomes ill or in immediate need. It may be losing certain liberties that we once took for granted, like walking into a government building without showing identification, going through metal detectors, or having our bags searched in the name of national, state, or local security.

Part 4: Lord, I Need Your Help!

Whether matters get better or worse, the end of the story brings a promising new beginning with God. Instead of looking to God to provide for us without any effort on our part, we can now take responsibility for our lives and whatever we accomplish to make for a more joyful and fulfilling life in God's kingdom for all whose lives He touched. His love was shared abundantly!

How bountiful are our blessings! When Jesus came to live on earth, He wrought miracles in abundance. His life on earth brought peace and joy to all whose lives He touched. His love was shared abundantly. After His death and resurrection, the church became firmly established and the truth of the gospel was made evident by its renewing power. The miracles were not nearly as frequent. Believers learned to walk by faith and not by sight. The acts of healing and deliverance were experienced in new ways. And the gospel has spread wherever God's children live. We hear the joyful sound: Jesus lives!

He still performs miracles. He still opens closed doors. While God provides manna in our wilderness and water during our seasons of desert travel, there comes a time when we need to do what our hands find to do. We will continue to make the best use of the resources God has given to us. God will do the rest. As it is sometimes said, "Man's extremities are God's opportunities."

When we could not save ourselves, God helped us. God sent us a Savior, Jesus, His only begotten son. Whether God provides by supernatural or by natural means, all of it is our most powerful Creator's will and way. When the manna ceases, we know that God may change His source of supply, but that no matter with what or when, God will always provide for his children's needs!

First, we have to live our lives under drastically changed conditions.

Second, things may get worse before they get better.

Third, we have a promising new beginning with God.

With God's Help…we will survive!

Decisive Decision Making
Robert E.C. Jones Jr.

"After this, Jesus went out and saw a tax collector named Levi sitting at the tax office, and he said to him, "Follow me." So, leaving everything behind, he got up and began to follow him."
Luke 5:27-28 (CSB)

During ancient biblical times, tax collectors were despised. Despised because they were social and religious outcasts who had chosen paths in life which separated them from a more meaningful and different purpose in life. Tax collectors were custom officials that were employed in Herod's civil office. Here in Luke 5:27-32 (cf. Matthew. 9:9-13; Mark. 2:13-17), we find a scene situated at Capernaum, and we read a short narrative wherein we find Levi. He was a tax collector—like a customs agent—charging and collecting import duties on wares brought through town as travelers made their way along important nearby trade routes. A tax collector held a very lucrative position. And the job as a tax collector provided security and prosperity. You see, tax collectors made wealthy wages. Not only did they collect for the government, but they often operated extorting their gains at times in illicit acts for their personal benefit. They, too, were persons unlikely to get their jobs back once they left, especially when leaving on short notice. Many tax collectors were at gateways where merchants and traders traveled cities and seaboards were heavily trafficked. So business was good. They lined their pockets with money.

In these biblical times, people regarded a person who was a man of wealth—and particularly if he was one who invited a religious teacher over for dinner—to be honorable in society. So, when Jesus announced that He was coming to dinner it was a noble gesture and a time for a big feast and celebration. Now, the guests expected would be the friends of Levi, most of whom were also tax collectors. However, tax collectors were regarded as collaborators with the Romans. So, they were despised by religious people in their day and were viewed as sinners not because they did not eat food of ritual purity, but because they lived a sinful life rather than a religious life. Tax collectors were also regarded as unwholesome individuals because as municipal aristocrats, their support of the Roman government was contrary to the interest of the Jewish population—many of whom were poor.

Levi, therefore, was seen to be someone with an unscrupulous character. But when Jesus calls Levi, he follows Him. There was much discontentment in the air. Moreover, Jesus' behavior ran counter to the standards of piety in the company of all His Jewish contemporaries.

Nonetheless, Levi responds to Jesus and he abandons his job to follow Him. He makes a very decisive decision—a decision that will undoubtedly change his life and future. To follow Jesus meant leaving everything—his job, his security, and whatever measure of popularity he may have had among those whom he did have as friends or close alliances. It meant putting himself in jeopardy whereas he would lose most of the material gains that made his life comfortable.

But, in a split moment when he heard the voice of Jesus, he realized he had a decisive decision to make. It was not a decision based on his material possessions, nor was it considered apropos by others. Some of his peers probably thought he was crazy. But Levi viewed his need to follow Jesus more important for the contentment of his soul. He made a choice. He chose to follow Jesus. He made an eternal decision—a decisive decision that rendered his possession of little value in comparison with the destiny of his soul and eternity.

Today, in our contemporary society, those who have made successful life and earnings must ask the question: What is more important? The wealth and riches to be had in the earth, or where time will be spent for eternity. Like Levi, the tax collectors were faced with a heart-centered decision. There are many people in our contemporary world who banish themselves from making a pointedly quick decision to follow Jesus when He calls. When Jesus calls, He calls those from a sin-sick world to a life of abundant victories and joy (Romans. 8:1; 1 John 1:4). And in such contemplation in one's decisive decision to follow the Lord, Jesus Christ, there is a better hope and promise for their tomorrow. When Jesus calls out "Follow Me," come running. And, like Levi, invite your friends too! Jesus comes for everybody. Most of all, He comes for those who are not well spiritually, but for all those who need a doctor—Dr. Jesus is His Name. Choose to follow Jesus when He calls your name. Be decisive, not indecisive. Jesus wants to use you.

Serving One Another
June A. Conner

"You, my brothers and sisters, were called to be free. But do not use your freedom to indulge the flesh; rather, serve one another humbly in love."

Galatians 5:13 (NIV)

As a school teacher in the Philadelphia School System, you run into some very disturbing situations. There was a student that I will never forget even though I worked for thirty-four years and have been retired for ten. We will call her Charlotte for the sake of this story.

Charlotte was a very thin, African American girl who was very fair with long jet black, wavy hair. Unlike some of my students, she came in dressed very nice, always neat and clean. She looked well cared for. She was in one of the kindergarten classes that came to me for music.

This particular kindergarten class had an excellent teacher who was well respected because her classes were always so disciplined and organized. Whenever she dropped her classes off for music, they were very well behaved, but this particular year she had this student, Charlotte, who was a handful.

Charlotte seemed angry all the time. She did not get along with the other children. She would snatch crayons or pencils from students while the class was working. If she did not get her way for any reason she would scream, a high pitched, very loud, scream. I had never heard a scream like that come from a child so small. She was not crying, she was just screaming, the kind of scream you hear in a horror movie when someone is being chased by a killer.

Unfortunately, once she started acting out, it took a while to calm her down. If she got angry enough, she was known to smack a child. Often, she had to be removed from the class because of her disruptive behavior, so she missed a lot of the schoolwork her class was doing.

No one seemed to know what was wrong with Charlotte. She was labeled mean, spoiled, and a "behavior problem." Her teachers thought that this was just because of poor parenting. They felt that she had not been taught any better, perhaps, because there was no mother in the home. I'm not sure why, but it was just Charlotte, her younger sister, and their father.

Because of her behavior, Charlotte did not do well in her classes and it was determined that she must repeat kindergarten. At the beginning of the next school year, Charlotte again walked into my music class. I could not help but notice Charlotte as she entered. First, because she walked in quietly and sat in her seat. But second, because when she looked up there were many, very deep black jagged marks and scratches all over her face, neck, and shoulders. It was

Part 4: Lord, I Need Your Help!

jarring because these black marks stood out starkly on her very light skin.

As the class progressed, Charlotte participated, was cooperative, and never once disrupted the class. There was no screaming or temper tantrums, but my mind was spinning wondering what she had been through that left her quiet and scarred.

When her teacher arrived, I whispered, "What happened to Charlotte?" She said, "Let me get them settled first, and then I'll talk to you." And then she told me one of the saddest stories that I had heard during my teaching career.

It seems that Charlotte was being sexually abused by her father. It was unclear how long the abuse had been going on, but they suspected it had been happening for quite some time. Charlotte had not told anyone so people around her had no idea what was going on in her young life. But one day, she walked into the bathroom of her home and found her father beginning to sexually abuse her younger sister. Charlotte grabbed her little sister and jumped through the closed plate glass bathroom window causing multiple cuts and gashes on her face, arms, and shoulders. This is how the adults in her life found out about the abuse. The school counselor surmised that she had endured it all through her first stint in kindergarten and probably even before that.

My mouth fell open as I walked from her classroom. I was dumbfounded. It was right there in front of us. This child had been screaming for help, but in a way that no one understood. Sexual child abuse at that time was not something you heard about; it definitely was not something people talked about. When she would have her screaming fits and act out, she was sent to the school counselor, or sent home, but no one suspected abuse. No one thought to look deeper into her "misbehavior." Of course, after this, she and her sister were removed from the home, entered into counseling, and was placed elsewhere.

The reason I remember her story so well is because it was early in my teaching career and I determined after that to really look at my students and actually "see" them; to look at their behavior and not make assumptions. If I thought I saw something that needed addressing, I would get involved. I referred students to the counselor and often talked to my students and their parents who seemed troubled. This taught me that we can't look at people and look through them and don't see the hurt or the pain that is often showing.

This not only happens with children but with adults. There are many people walking around with huge burdens, depressed and upset, just looking for a kind word, while we keep it moving. A few years back, we had a pastor friend, who pastored a small church in Philadelphia, who everyone thought was doing fine until he walked into his church one day, locked the door to his office, and blew himself away. No one knew he was hurting. He had a wife and children who were shocked. Our goal as Christians is to help alleviate some of the pain in the world and to be of service to others. We cannot do that if we are so wrapped in what we are going through that we don't see anyone else.

Part 4: Lord, I Need Your Help!

The scripture says to, "Serve one another humbly in love!" Let us pray for the spirit of God to give us the grace and the power of discernment to take time with people to see what is going on in their lives and hear their stories. Let's not wait until someone has to jump through a plate glass window or lock themselves in their office to get our attention.

Like Rizpah
Audrey E. Moody

"And Rizpah the daughter of Aiah took sackcloth and spread it for herself on the rock...and she allowed neither the birds of the sky to rest on them by day nor the beasts of the field by night."
2 Samuel 21:10 (NASB).

On safari in South Africa in October 2015, I looked on with many others, at a lion crouched in front of a distant tree. In the foreground, lay the decimated carcass of a giraffe—mutilated, dismembered.

We just looked. There were several cars and jeeps, full of tourists and their native guides. We all had our devices—cameras, cell phones, iPads, tablets—focused intently and alternately on the lion and on the giraffe. Earlier that morning, we learned that around 5 a.m., the lion had successfully stalked and slaughtered the giraffe. When he was finished, the lion sauntered back to the shade of the distant tree. As we continued to look on, the lion roused himself and walked toward the giraffe and toward those of us who sat safely in our cars and jeeps. With a steady gaze, the lion seemed to speak to us:

Oh Lord, Why Me?

Yeah, I did it! Yeah, I am big and bold and bad! Yeah, I am the king of the jungle!

Yeah, I do what I want to do! Yeah, and what are you going to do about it?

This reminds me of George Floyd with a knee on his neck; of Ahmed Asberry jogging in his neighborhood; of Rayshawn Brooks sleeping off a drunk in a Wendy's drive thru; of Breonna Taylor sleeping in her own bed…and all the others…all killed at the hands of an unjust police system. Yeah, and what are we going to do about it?

African American men and women whose names we know; names we say out loud. Names of our sons and daughters; our sisters and brothers and fathers and mothers. Our names.

Justin Powell	Sean Monterrosa	Sandra Bland
Jamel Floyd	Michael Brown	Tamir Rice
Botham Jean	Trayvon Martin	

Do we take just pictures? Do we look on in curiosity? Do we stand by helplessly?

Or do we take action like Rizpah, refusing to give up our sons and daughters to an unjust system, beating the vultures away from the bodies of her dead children, with a fierce determination, wanting God's justice for God's people.

Part 4: Lord, I Need Your Help!

I think of the viral video of the mother who demanded that her son leave that crowd of looters and dragged him away. I think of the mother who went to the drug house in the dead of night and pulled her son out. I think of the father who drove all night to rescue his daughter from her abusive husband.

Rizpah stood her ground on behalf of her sons and daughters, and exhibited courage, tenacity, determination, commitment, and, yes, even sacrifice.

"And Rizpah the daughter of Aiah took sackcloth and spread it for herself on the rock…and she allowed neither the birds of the sky to rest on them by day nor the beasts of the field by night." (2 Samuel 21:10 NASB).

www.ingramcontent.com/pod-product-compliance
Lightning Source LLC
Chambersburg PA
CBHW071025080526
44587CB00015B/2510